EXPLORING CONTINENTS

AFRICA

Deborah Underwood

Heinemann LIBRARY

www.heinemann.co.uk/library
Visit our website to find out more information about Heinemann Library books.

To order:
☎ Phone 44 (0) 1865 888066
🖹 Send a fax to 44 (0) 1865 314091
🖥 Visit the Heinemann Bookshop at www.heinemann.co.uk/library to browse our catalogue and order online.

First published in Great Britain by Heinemann, Halley Court, Jordan Hill, Oxford, OX2 8EJ, part of Harcourt Education.

Editorial: Louise Galpine and Harriet Milles
Design: Richard Parker and Q2A Solutions
Illustrations: Jeff Edwards
Picture Research: Mica Brancic and Beatrice Ray
Production: Camilla Crask

Originated by Chroma
Printed and bound in China by WKT

10 digit ISBN 0 431 09742 9 (hardback)
13 digit ISBN 978 0 431 09742 8 (hardback)

11 10 09 08 07
10 9 8 7 6 5 4 3 2 1

British Library Cataloguing in Publication Data
Underwood, Deborah
  Africa. - (Exploring continents)
  1.Africa - Geography - Juvenile literature
  I.Title
  916
A full catalogue record for this book is available from the British Library.

Acknowledgements
The publishers would like to thank the following for permission to reproduce photographs: Corbis pp. **16** (Joe McDonald), **21** (Bettmann), **22** (SIME); Getty pp. **5** (National Geographic), **7** (Stone), **8** (Photographer's Choice), **9** (Photonica), **11** (Photographer's Choice), **12** (Photographer's Choice), **13** (Gallo Images), **14** (Taxi/Anup Shah), **15** (Image Bank), **18** Science Photo Library/Sam Ogden, **19** (Image Bank), **24** (Image Bank), **23** Network Photographers, **25** (Image Bank), **27**.

Cover satellite image of Africa reproduced with permission of SPL/M-Sat Ltd.

Every effort has been made to contact copyright holders of any material reproduced in this book. Any omissions will be rectified in subsequent printings if notice is given to the publisher.

CONTENTS

Words that appear in the text in bold, **like this**, are explained in the Glossary.

WHAT IS A CONTINENT?

Land on Earth is divided into seven large areas. These areas of land are called continents. Continents are the largest units of land on Earth. The continents are called Africa, Antarctica, Asia, Australia, Europe, North America, and South America.

Millions of years ago, the continents were all joined together. They formed a huge **land mass** named Pangaea. Over time, Earth's **crust** shifted. The land mass broke into pieces. These pieces slowly drifted apart and became the continents we know today.

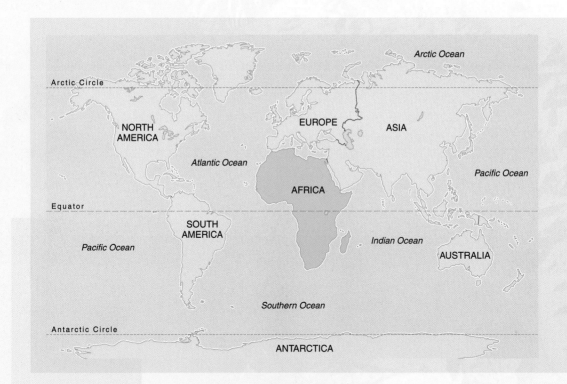

This map shows the world's seven continents.

Did you know?

On most maps, the continents can look bigger or smaller than they really are. While North America and Africa may look about the same size, Africa is more than 5.2 million square kilometres (2 million square miles) larger than North America!

The continent of Africa

Africa is the world's second largest continent, after Asia. Asia and Africa are connected by a small piece of land named the Sinai **Peninsula**. Oceans and seas surround Africa. The Atlantic Ocean laps at its west coast. The Mediterranean Sea and Red Sea can be found off its northern coasts. Africa's east coast meets the Indian Ocean.

Africa includes a number of islands. Madagascar lies off Africa's southeast coast. At 592,800 square kilometres (228,821 square miles), Madagascar is almost the size of Spain and Denmark put together.

HOW BIG IS AFRICA?

- *Land area:* 30,365,000 square kilometres (11,720,000 square miles)

- *Distance north to south:* 8,000 kilometres (5,000 miles)

- *Distance east to west:* 7,500 kilometres (4,700 miles) at widest point

Africa is famous for its vast areas of grassland and fascinating wildlife.

WHAT DOES AFRICA LOOK LIKE?

Africa has many types of landscape. They include vast deserts, sweeping **savannahs**, and lush rainforests. East Africa has lots of mountains and lakes. Woodlands and grassy plains cover much of Africa's centre.

High and low

Most of Africa is made up of **plateaus**. These plateaus are large, high, and mostly flat. The highest plateaus are in the east and south. This area is called High Africa. Most of High Africa is more than 910 metres (3,000 feet) above sea level. The rest of the country makes up Low Africa. Low Africa ranges from 150 to 610 metres (500 to 2,000 feet) above sea level.

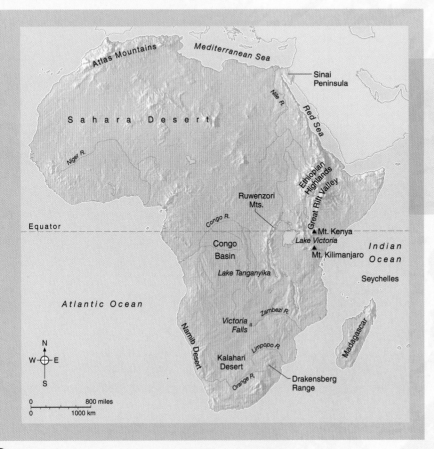

This map shows the main landscape features of Africa.

Africa's Great Rift Valley is about 6,400 kilometres (4,000 miles) long, and up to 100 kilometres (60 miles) wide.

Mountains

Africa does not have many mountain ranges. The Atlas Mountains are in northern Africa. The Ethiopian Highlands are to the east and the Drakensberg Range sits near the southern tip of the continent. The Ruwenzori Mountains can be found alongside the Great Rift Valley.

The highest peaks in Africa do not belong to mountain ranges. Mount Kilimanjaro and Mount Kenya are the tallest mountains in Africa. Both are **extinct** volcanoes. They rise out of the Great Rift Valley.

Deserts

The Sahara Desert stretches across northern Africa and is the largest desert in the world. Sand dunes cover about 25 per cent of the Sahara. The rest of the desert is made of rocks and gravel.

The long Namib Desert runs along Africa's southwestern coast. It is 1,900 kilometres (1,200 miles) long, but only 130 to 160 kilometres (80 to 100 miles) wide. The northern Namib is made of gravel plains. The south is brick-red sands.

The Kalahari Desert in southern Africa is connected to the Namib and is mostly covered in sand. White **salt pans** shimmer in the north where a huge lake stood thousands of years ago. When the climate changed and the lake dried up, only the salts from its water remained.

Sand dunes in the Sahara Desert can stretch for miles.

Did you know?

Millions of years ago, animals gathered at lakes in the Great Rift Valley. When the animals died, layers of soil and ash from erupting volcanoes buried their bones. As Earth's crust shifted, the bones were brought back up to the surface. Many important **fossils** have been discovered in the Great Rift Valley.

Lakes and rivers

Africa's largest lakes can be found in the Great Rift Valley. Lake Victoria is the world's second-largest freshwater lake. It is nearly as big as Scotland! Nearby Lake Tanganyika is the second-deepest lake in the world.

Africa is also home to the world's longest river. The River Nile flows north from Lake Victoria, and empties into the Mediterranean Sea. The Niger, Congo, and Zambezi are other major African rivers.

AFRICA LANDSCAPE FACTS:

- *Tallest mountain:* Mount Kilimanjaro 5,895 metres (19,340 feet)
- *Largest desert:* Sahara 8,600,000 square kilometres (3,320,000 square miles)
- *Longest river:* Nile 6,695 kilometres (4,160 miles)
- *Largest lake:* Lake Victoria 69,484 square kilometres (26,828 square miles)

The Zambezi River pours over a steep cliff to form the famous Victoria Falls. The Falls lie on the **border** between Zambia and Zimbabwe.

WHAT IS AFRICA'S CLIMATE LIKE?

The **equator** cuts through the middle of the continent, so Africa's climate is mostly warm or hot. However, temperatures become lower at high **altitudes**. This means weather in Africa's mountain areas can be cold. Even though Mount Kilimanjaro is near the equator, its peak is capped with ice all year long.

Most of Africa falls into four major climate zones. From driest to wettest, the zones are **arid**, semi-arid, tropical dry, and tropical wet.

Africa's arid places are its deserts. Most of these areas receive less than 250 mm (10 inches) of rain per year. Daytime temperatures can be higher than 41°C (105°F), while night temperatures may drop below 0°C (32°F).

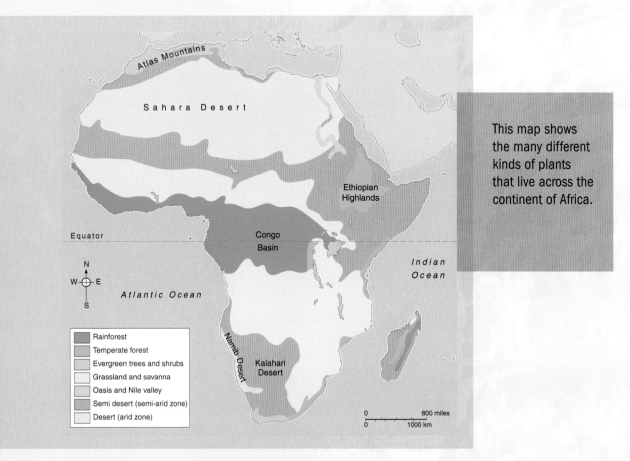

This map shows the many different kinds of plants that live across the continent of Africa.

Rainforest
Temperate forest
Evergreen trees and shrubs
Grassland and savanna
Oasis and Nile valley
Semi desert (semi-arid zone)
Desert (arid zone)

Semi-arid zones separate Africa's deserts from tropical areas. Semi-arid regions usually get 250 to 510 mm (10 to 20 inches) of rain per year. Temperatures range from below 0°C (32°F) to more than 38°C (100°F).

Tropical dry places have at least one wet season every year when much of their rain falls. Annual rainfall ranges from 510 to 1,520 mm (20 to 60 inches). Temperatures are hot all year. In some places, daily high temperatures average more than 32°C (90°F).

Africa's tropical wet areas are near the equator. They get lots of rainfall and are always hot, with average temperatures of more than 27°C (81°F). Some places receive more than 3,810 mm (150 inches) of rain per year. Rain falls all year, but is heavier in some months than in others.

The wettest rainforest areas can get more than 10,160 mm (400 inches) of rain per year.

HIGHS AND LOWS:

◉ Africa's highest recorded temperature was 58°C (136°F) at Al Aziziyah, Libya in 1922.

◎ Buffelsfontein in South Africa reached a lowest temperature of -18°C (0°F) in 2005.

WHAT PLANTS AND ANIMALS LIVE IN AFRICA?

Africa has many different climates and landscapes, so a wide range of plants and animals can live there. Some can be found all over the continent. Others live only in certain areas.

Date palms, fig trees, and shrubs are among the plants that might be found growing in an oasis.

Plant life

Many plants have ways to survive the fierce heat and dry air of African deserts. Some have roots that reach more than 40 metres (130 feet) into the earth to find hidden water. Others store water for later use.

An island of green in a desert marks the presence of an **oasis**. In these spots, underground water comes near the surface.

In central Africa's rainforests, plants get plenty of water. Rainforests have a great variety of plant life, including mahogany trees, orchids, and African violets.

Desert animals

Deserts may look empty, but they are full of life.
Scarab beetles scuttle across sands. Slithering snakes
hunt for rodents. Desert hedgehogs peek out from
underground burrows. More than 300 types of bird
spend some time each year in the Sahara.

Like desert plants, desert animals have ways
to survive the hot, dry climate. Camels can go
many days without drinking. Scorpions hide in
the desert sand while the sun is out. Tiny fennec
foxes have large ears that let heat escape from
their bodies quickly.

Cobras can be found
living in extremely
dry conditions.

On the savannah

Many types of animals make their homes on Africa's grassy plains and woodlands. During the dry season, some of these animals move closer to water holes to find the most tender plants. When rains come, the animals spread out again.

Giraffes are some of Africa's most recognizable animals. Their long necks allow them to eat tasty leaves high in the trees. The only other large animals on the savannah who can reach high leaves are elephants.

Giraffes use their long tongue to reach the leaves they eat.

Dozens of types of **antelope** roam the savannahs.
Elands, duikers, impalas, nyalas, wildebeest, and
dikdiks are all types of antelope. They vary greatly
in size. An eland can weigh more than 10 people
put together. The tiny dik-dik weighs only 4.5 to 5.5
kilograms (10 to 12 pounds) – the same as a pet cat!

Africa's **carnivores** eat other animals. They rely on
bursts of speed to catch their prey. Cheetahs can
reach top speeds of 113 kilometres (70 miles) per
hour! Other African carnivores include lions, wild dogs,
and spotted hyenas.

A cheetah closes in on
a Thompson's gazelle.

Did you know?

Every year in East Africa, more than one million wildebeest, zebras,
and gazelles begin their annual **migration**. They leave dry areas and
move in a circular path looking for fresh grasses to eat. They travel
more than 1,287 kilometres (800 miles) a year.

Rainforest creatures

Many of Africa's rainforest animals are found nowhere else on Earth. The rare pygmy hippopotamus lives near swamps and rivers. It measures only about 1.5 metres (5 feet) long. The okapi looks like a zebra, but it is really related to the giraffe. It has a rich brown coat, with white stripes on its legs. Chimpanzees live in Africa's rainforests and woodlands. Gorillas live in rainforests and mountain areas near the equator.

The fates of Africa's plants and animals are tied together. Forests shrink as people cut down trees to get wood or to clear land for crops. Chimpanzees, gorillas, and others who dwell in these forests are losing their homes.

If the African forests are not saved, animals, such as these gorillas, will vanish from the wild forever.

WHAT ARE AFRICA'S NATURAL RESOURCES?

Africa is rich in natural resources. Diamonds, gold, and oil are just a few of the resources hidden deep in Africa's soil. The most valuable **minerals** come from a small handful of countries.

Most of Africa's oil comes from two areas: north Africa, and the west coast of central Africa. The country of Nigeria produces the most oil. Libya, Algeria, Angola, and Egypt are other major producers.

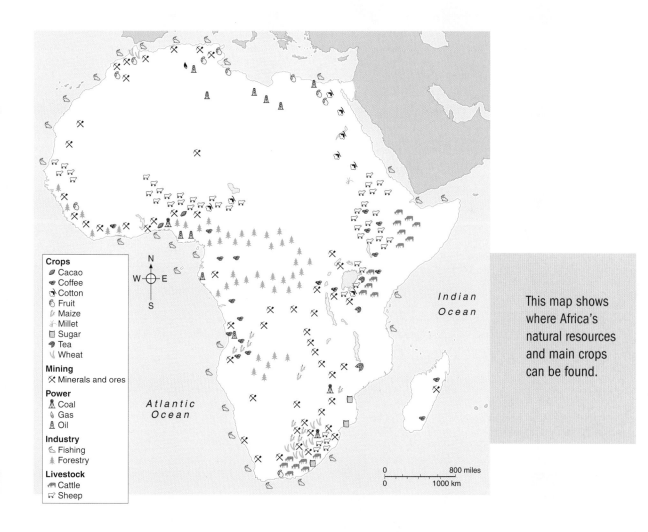

Crops
- Cacao
- Coffee
- Cotton
- Fruit
- Maize
- Millet
- Sugar
- Tea
- Wheat

Mining
- Minerals and ores

Power
- Coal
- Gas
- Oil

Industry
- Fishing
- Forestry

Livestock
- Cattle
- Sheep

Indian Ocean

Atlantic Ocean

0   800 miles
0   1000 km

This map shows where Africa's natural resources and main crops can be found.

Mineral wealth

Many precious metals and gems are mined in Africa. The country of South Africa produces more gold than any other country in the world. Around half of the world's diamonds come from Africa. Botswana mines more diamonds than any other African country.

Africa produces many other minerals, too. Guinea has over one-third of the world's **reserves** of bauxite, which is used to make aluminium. A large share of the world's phosphate reserves are in Morocco. Phosphate is used to make fertilizer.

With all of Africa's valuable resources, it seems the African people would be rich. However, the money produced by oil and minerals does not reach most of Africa's people. A large number of Africans live on less than 56 pence a day.

High-quality diamonds are used in fine jewellery. Others are used in industry.

Africa's agriculture

Agriculture is the most important business in Africa. Some people grow food to feed themselves. Others grow plants that they can sell to make money. These plants are called **cash crops**.

Many people in **rural** areas rely on farming to feed their families. They might grow bananas, rice, **maize**, yams, or **cassava**. In many parts of Africa, however, rain may not fall for a long period of time. During these **droughts**, crops die and people go hungry. These **famines** kill thousands of people.

West Africa grows nearly 70 per cent of the world's cacao beans. The beans are sold to Europe and North America. Companies turn them into cocoa and other chocolate items. Other African cash crops include peanuts, cotton, coffee, and tea.

More farmers are choosing to grow cash crops. However, when too many farmers stop growing food, it leads to food shortages.

After cacao beans are picked, they are aged, dried, and roasted.

Did you know?

Traders and camel **caravans** cross the desert to get a mineral we take for granted: salt. They load heavy slabs of salt onto their camels. Then they journey for days to reach towns where the salt can be sold.

WHAT COUNTRIES AND CITIES ARE IN AFRICA?

Africa is divided into 54 different countries. Many of the borders between countries were decided on more than 100 years ago. People from Europe, not Africa, created these borders.

Africa's countries

The countries of Western Sahara, Morocco, Algeria, Tunisia, Libya, and Egypt are sometimes known as North Africa. The other African countries together are called sub-Saharan Africa, because they are located south of the Sahara desert.

This map shows Africa's countries and their capital cities.

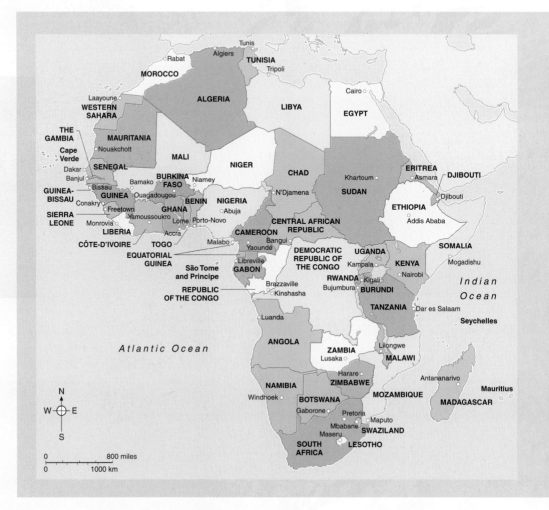

Africa's colonial past

In the late 1800s, countries in Europe wanted Africa's land and resources. They divided Africa among themselves. For decades, European countries ruled most of Africa. When one nation controls another one in this way, it is called **colonialism**.

Most African countries did not gain their **independence** until the 1950s and 1960s. The new president of Tanzania, Julius Nyerere, celebrates on the day Tanzania won its independence.

COUNTRY FACTS:

- Largest country: Sudan 2,505,813 square kilometres (967,500 square miles)
- Smallest country: Seychelles 455 square kilometres (176 square miles)
- Largest population: Nigeria 136,769,000 people
- Smallest population: Seychelles 84,000 people

Africa's cities

About 40 per cent of Africa's people live in **urban** areas. Some cities are modern, but many Africans live without running water or electricity. In rural places, only about one person in fifty has electric power. Even in some cities, power is not reliable.

Cairo, Egypt's capital, sits on the banks of the River Nile. It is Africa's largest city, with nearly 11 million people. People shop at the city's open-air markets and sip coffee at outdoor cafes. The city's Egyptian Museum displays items from thousands of years of Egypt's history.

Nairobi, the capital of Kenya, is a city of contrasts. Part of the city is modern, with schools, parks, and museums. However, more than half of Nairobi's people are poor. Kibera, which is part of Nairobi, is one of the world's largest **slums**. In Kibera, nearly one million people live in metal shacks with dirt floors and no running water.

In Cairo, tall, slender towers called minarets rise above the city's **mosques**.

WHO LIVES IN AFRICA?

Africa is a land of many **cultures**. More than 900 million people live in Africa. The continent is home to more than 1,000 **ethnic groups**. People in an ethnic group share a language and a way of life.

More than 1,500 languages are spoken in Africa. But the official language of many African countries is English, French, or Portuguese. This is left over from the days when European countries controlled Africa.

Colonialism brought problems that still exist. Some borders split tribes of people between two or more countries. Others put groups that did not get along with each other into the same country.

Many Africans live in large cities, such as Nairobi, the capital of Kenya.

Culture and religion

North of the Sahara, Arabs make up the largest ethnic group. In most of northern Africa, people speak Arabic. The main religion here is Islam. People who practise Islam are known as Muslims.

In sub-Saharan Africa, there are hundreds of different cultures. Kiswahili, Hausa, Fulfude, Yoruba, and Igbo are some languages that are spoken. Many sub-Saharan Africans practise **native** religions. Christianity and Islam are also widespread.

The Tuareg people live in the Sahara Desert. Men wrap their heads in a cloth called a *tagelmust*. This protects them from blowing sand and the harsh desert sun. In the past, Tuareg traders carried goods across the desert on their camels. Some Tuareg people still live this way today, although many have become modern farmers instead.

The Tuareg are sometimes known as the "blue men of the desert". This is because the blue dye from their clothing rubs off on their skin.

The Dogon people live in Mali. Most of them live in a place called Bandiagara, at the base of high sandstone cliffs. Their mud homes and **granaries** blend in with the cliffs that tower above. The Dogon are farmers who grow **millet**, **sorghum**, onions, and other foods. Tribal members perform masked dances that are an important part of their culture.

The Fulani people live in many west African countries. In the past, as cattle herders, they lived a **nomadic** lifestyle. Many continue to move from place to place to find good **grazing** land for their animals. Others have settled on farms or in cities.

In the Democratic Republic of Congo's rainforest, the Mbuti **Pygmies** live in leaf-covered huts. They gather plants to eat, and hunt small animals with bows, arrows, and nets. They trade meat for aluminium pots, cloth, and grains. They move from place to place in the forest, making new homes with each move. Music and storytelling are important to their culture.

The Dogon people honour the spirits of the dead in a special celebration called a dama.

WHAT FAMOUS PLACES ARE IN AFRICA?

Natural wonders

Victoria Falls lies on the border between Zambia and Zimbabwe, where the Zambezi River plunges off a steep cliff. When the river is high, the falls are more than 1.6 kilometres (one mile) wide.

Kruger National Park in South Africa is a great area for viewing wildlife. Tourists come to see lions, elephants, and many other animals. The animals in the park are protected from hunters.

This map shows where some of Africa's famous landmarks can be found.

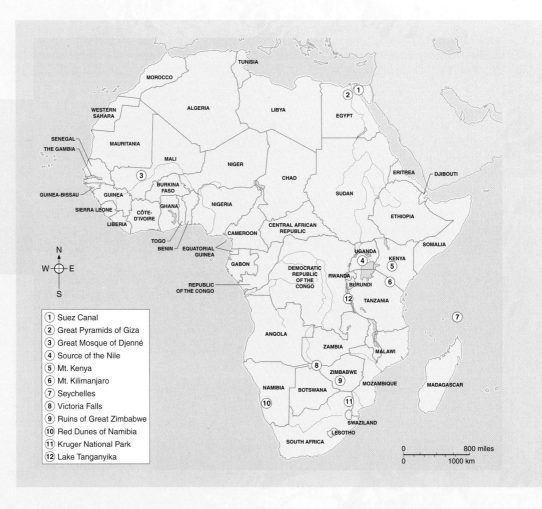

1. Suez Canal
2. Great Pyramids of Giza
3. Great Mosque of Djenné
4. Source of the Nile
5. Mt. Kenya
6. Mt. Kilimanjaro
7. Seychelles
8. Victoria Falls
9. Ruins of Great Zimbabwe
10. Red Dunes of Namibia
11. Kruger National Park
12. Lake Tanganyika

Ancient remains

Egypt's famous pyramids were built thousands of years ago. The Great Pyramid at Giza, near Cairo, is made up of about two million blocks of stone. Scientists believe some of the stones were pulled from 800 kilometres (500 miles) away!

The ruins of Great Zimbabwe are some of sub-Saharan Africa's oldest structures. The city was once home to 12,000 people. It was abandoned more than 500 years ago for unknown reasons.

Modern landmarks

The Suez Canal in Egypt links the Mediterranean Sea to the Red Sea. Before the canal was built, ships from Europe had to sail all the way around Africa to reach Asia. The canal, which is 163 kilometres (101 miles) long, was finished in 1869.

The Great Mosque at Djenné in Mali is the largest mud brick building in the world. It was built in 1907 on the site of a mosque from the 1200s. Each year, people climb up the walls to add more mud.

Each spring during a festival, the townspeople work together to prepare more mud to put on the walls of the Great Mosque at Djenné.

27

CONTINENTS COMPARISON CHART

Continent	Area	Population	
AFRICA	30,365,000 square kilometres (11,720,000 square miles)	906 million	
ANTARCTICA	14,200,000 square kilometres (5,500,000 square miles)	officially none, but about 4,000 people live on the research stations during the summer and over 3,000 people visit as tourists each year. People have lived there for as long as three and a half years at a time.	
ASIA	44,614,000 square kilometres (17,226,200 square miles)	almost 4,000 million	
AUSTRALIA	7,713,364 square kilometres (2,966,136 square miles)	approximately 20,090,400 (2005 estimate)	
EUROPE	10,400,000 square kilometres (4,000,000 square miles)	approximately 727 million (2005 estimate)	
NORTH AMERICA	24,230,000 square kilometres (9,355,000 square miles)	approximately 509,915,000 (2005 estimate)	
SOUTH AMERICA	17,814,000 square kilometres (6,878,000 square miles)	380 million	

Number of countries	Highest point	Longest river
54 (includes Western Sahara)	Mount Kilimanjaro, Tanzania — 5,895 metres (19,340 feet)	River Nile — 6,695 kilometres (4,160 miles)
none, but over 23 countries have research stations in Antarctica	Vinson Massif — 4,897 metres (16,067 feet)	Onyx River — 12 kilometres (7.5 miles) **Biggest ice shelf** Ross Ice Shelf in western Antarctica — 965 kilometres (600 miles) long.
50	Mount Everest, Tibet and Nepal — 8,850 metres (29,035 feet)	Yangtze River, China — 6,300 kilometres (3,914 miles)
1	Mount Kosciusko — 2,229 metres (7,313 feet)	Murray River — 2,520 kilometres (1,566 miles)
47	Mount Elbrus, Russia — 5,642 metres (18,510 feet)	Volga River — 3,685 kilometres (2,290 miles)
23	Mount McKinley (Denali) in Alaska — 6,194 metres (20,320 feet)	Mississippi/Missouri River System — 6,270 kilometres (3,895 miles)
12	Aconcagua, Argentina — 6,959 metres (22,834 feet)	River Amazon — 6,400 kilometres (4,000 miles)

GLOSSARY

agriculture growing crops and raising livestock

altitude height

antelope type of horned animal that runs quickly

arid dry

border imaginary line separating two geographic areas (such as countries)

caravan group of people travelling together

carnivore animal that eats other animals

cash crop plant grown to be sold for money

cassava plant with a starchy root that can be eaten

colonialism ruling of one country by another

crust Earth's rocky outer shell

culture customs and ideas that a group of people passes on to its children and grandchildren

drought long period with no rainfall

equator imaginary line around the middle of the earth

ethnic group group of people that shares a common culture and history

extinct no longer living or active

famine food shortage

fossil ancient remains of an animal or plant that has been dug from the earth

granary building for storing grain

graze feed on growing grasses or leaves

independence freedom from control by others

land mass large area of land

maize food crop also known as corn

migration group of animals moving from one place to another during a certain season

millet grass that produces small seeds that can be eaten

mineral naturally occurring substance taken from the ground for human use

mosque Muslim place of worship

native to come from or belong to a particular region or area

nomadic moving from place to place

oasis area in a desert where underground wells or springs are close to the surface so plants can grow

peninsula piece of land almost surrounded by water

plateau high, mostly flat area of land

Pygmy member of one of the small-statured peoples of Africa. Some are known as Bushmen or San.

reserves amount of a mineral known to exist but not yet taken out of the land

rural country areas

salt pan area of dry salt where there was once salt water

savannah flat grassland

slum part of a city that is known for its poverty and poor living conditions

sorghum type of grass from which a sweet syrup can be made

urban city areas

FURTHER INFORMATION

Books

All About Continents series, Bruce McClish (Heinemann Library, 2004)

Country Files: South Africa, Ian Graham (Franklin Watts Ltd, 2004)

Cultural Journeys: Traditions from Africa, Vivien Golding, Joan Amin-Addo
  (Hodder Wayland, 2000)

Journey into Africa, Tim Knight (Photographer), (Oxford University Press, 2002)

Landscapes and People: *Earth's changing continents*, Neil Morris (Raintree, 2004)

Useful websites

* A site containing lots of information and some beautiful pictures of Africa:
  http://www.nationalgeographic.com/africa/
* A site with a clickable map of Africa and lots of links to other websites:
  http://www.africaguide.com/afmap.htm
* The website of the African Wildlife Foundation contains lots of information about
  the amazing animals in Africa. You can even listen to what some of them sound like:
  http://www.awf.org/
* A well-organized guide to Africa:
  http://www.worldtravelguide.net/country/countries.ehtml?o=1

Disclaimer

All the internet addresses (URLs) given in this book were valid at the time of going to
press. However, due to the dynamic nature of the internet, some addresses may have
changed, or sites may have ceased to exist since publication. While the author and
publishers regret any inconvenience this may cause readers, no responsibility for such
changes can be accepted by either the author(s) or the publishers.

INDEX

Titles in the Exploring Continents series include:

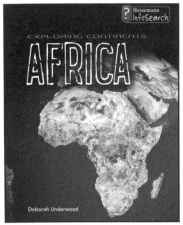

Hardback   0 431 09742 9

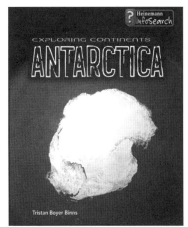

Hardback   0 431 09743 7

Hardback   0 431 09744 5

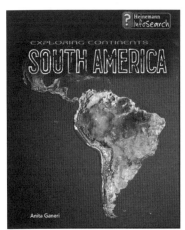

Hardback   0 431 09745 3

Hardback   0 431 09746 1

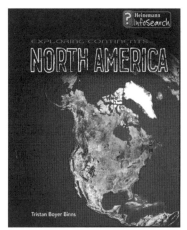

Hardback   0 431 09747 X

Hardback   0 431 09748 8

Find out about other titles from Heinemann Library on our website www.heinemann.co.uk/library